D0778705

SEP 1 4

African Animals

Zebras

ABDO
Publishing Company

Big
Buddy BOOKS
African Animals

by Julie Murray

Published by ABDO Publishing Company, PO Box 398166, Minneapolis, MN 55439.

Printed in the United States of America, North Mankato, Minnesota.
102011
012012

 PRINTED ON RECYCLED PAPER

Coordinating Series Editor: Rochelle Baltzer
Editor: Marcia Zappa
Contributing Editors: Megan M. Gunderson, BreAnn Rumsch, Sarah Tieck
Graphic Design: Maria Hosley
Cover Photograph: *Shutterstock*: Donovan van Staden
Interior Photographs/Illustrations: *Corbis* (p. 8); *iStockphoto*: ©iStockphoto.com/brytta (p. 4), ©iStockphoto.com/
    PTB-images (p. 4); *Minden Pictures*: Sergey Gorshkov (p. 23); *Photolibrary*: Age fotostock (p. 15), Bios
    (pp. 7, 21), Cusp (p. 13), Oxford Scientific (OSF) (p. 17), Mueller R (p. 21), Peter Arnold Images (pp. 7, 13, 27),
    Jonathan & Angela Scott (p. 19), Still Pictures (p. 25); *Shutterstock*: Galyna Andrushko (p. 9), Baloncici (p. 9),
    Paul Banton (p. 11), Eric Isselée (p. 14), Mackland (p. 13), Dave Pusey (p. 7), Graeme Shannon (p. 9), Johan
    Swanepoel (pp. 8, 25); *Stockbyte* (pp. 5, 29).

Library of Congress Cataloging-in-Publication Data

Murray, Julie, 1969-.
 Zebras / Julie Murray.
    p. cm. -- (African animals)
 ISBN 978-1-61783-222-2
 1. Zebras--Juvenile literature. I. Title.
 QL737.U62M875 2012
 599.665'7--dc23
                        2011028361

Contents

Long ago, nearly all land on Earth was one big mass. About 200 million years ago, the land began to break into **continents**. One of these is called Africa.

Zebras are members of the horse family. They are known for their black and white stripes.

Africa is the second-largest continent. It is known for hot weather, wild land, and interesting animals. One of these animals is the zebra. In the wild, zebras are only found in Africa.

Zebra Territory

There are three types of zebras. These are plains zebras, Grevy's zebras, and mountain zebras.

Plains zebras live mostly in southern and eastern Africa. Their **habitat** is grasslands and open woodlands.

Grevy's zebras prefer dry grasslands and deserts. They live in small areas of eastern Africa.

Mountain zebras are found in southern Africa. They live on **plateaus** and mountains.

SAHARA DESERT

Nile River

Plains Zebra Territory

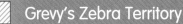
Grevy's Zebra Territory

Mountain Zebra Territory

Grevy's zebras

mountain zebras

plains zebras

Jambo! Welcome to Africa!

If you took a trip to where zebras live, you might find…

…many languages.

More than 1,000 languages are spoken across Africa! Swahili (swah-HEE-lee) is common in southern Africa where zebras live. In Swahili, *jambo* is a greeting for visitors. *Masalala* means "goodness!" or "wow!" And *punda milia* means "zebra."

…grasslands.

About one-third of Africa is covered in grasslands. Many animals live in these areas. They include elephants, giraffes, lions, and zebras.

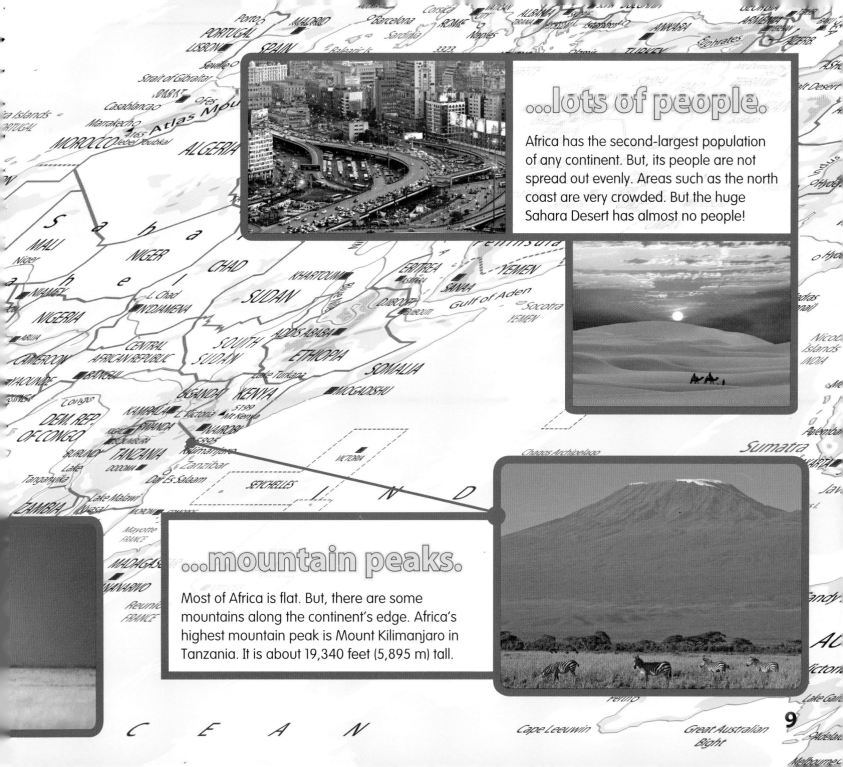

...lots of people.

Africa has the second-largest population of any continent. But, its people are not spread out evenly. Areas such as the north coast are very crowded. But the huge Sahara Desert has almost no people!

...mountain peaks.

Most of Africa is flat. But, there are some mountains along the continent's edge. Africa's highest mountain peak is Mount Kilimanjaro in Tanzania. It is about 19,340 feet (5,895 m) tall.

Take a Closer Look

Zebras have horselike bodies. Their thin legs are strong. And, they have hard hooves for feet. Zebras have long faces with large ears. Their eyes are on the sides of their faces.

Adult zebras are 3.5 to 5 feet (1.1 to 1.5 m) tall at their shoulders. They weigh 440 to 990 pounds (200 to 450 kg).

A zebra can turn its ears to listen for danger.

Sensational Stripes

Zebras are easily recognized by their bold coats. Most zebras have a white base coat with dark brown or black stripes. A few have a dark base coat with white stripes.

No two zebras have exactly the same pattern. But, zebras of the same type look similar.

Uncovered!
Zebras have solid black skin under their fur.

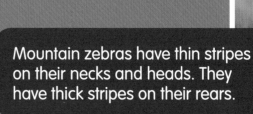

Mountain zebras have thin stripes on their necks and heads. They have thick stripes on their rears.

A Grevy's zebra has thin stripes except for one wide stripe running down its back.

Some plains zebras have lighter stripes between their main stripes. These are called shadow stripes.

Scientists have several ideas about why zebras have stripes. Some believe stripes help zebras recognize one another. This may help herds of zebras stay together.

Many scientists believe zebra stripes help guard against predators. When zebras stand together, their stripes make it hard to tell them apart. Stripes may also make it hard for a predator to tell how far away a zebra is.

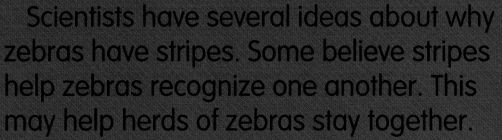

The short, stiff mane on a zebra's neck is striped like its body.

Predators prefer to pick just one animal to attack. The stripes on zebras make this hard to do.

15

Mealtime

Zebras are **herbivores**. They eat mostly grass. They also eat leaves, bark, fruit, buds, and roots.

Zebras spend many hours each day eating. They use their sharp front teeth to bite plants. Then, they use their dull back teeth to grind up food.

A zebra's teeth never stop growing. Eating hard plants wears them down so they don't get too long.

Herd Life

Zebras are **social** animals. Most live together in family groups with one male, several females, and their young. Young males form groups of their own.

Often, groups of zebras join together to form large herds. Zebra herds move around together searching for food and water.

Zebra herds can have several hundred members!

Uncovered!

Grevy's zebras usually live on their own instead of in groups or herds. Male Grevy's zebras use their pee and poop to mark territories. Females and young zebras move around freely.

Zebras **communicate** with each other in many ways. They make sounds including barks, snorts, and brays. Zebras use their eyes, ears, and mouths to make meaningful faces. They also communicate by **grooming** each other.

Male zebras sometimes fight over females. They may push, bite, or kick each other.

When zebras groom each other, it may look like they are biting. But, they are actually pulling out loose hairs with their teeth.

Uncovered!
Male zebras are called stallions. Females are called mares.

Staying Safe

Zebras have many predators. They stay safe by keeping together in family groups and herds. Zebras take turns resting and eating. That way, one is always watching for danger.

When predators attack, zebras usually try to run away. Zebras can run up to 40 miles (64 km) per hour! If they can't run away, family groups work together to **protect** their members. They may bite or kick predators.

A zebra's predators include lions (*below*), hyenas, cheetahs, leopards, crocodiles, and wild dogs.

Uncovered!
Adult males often stay behind their family groups. They try to stop predators from reaching the others.

Baby Zebras

Zebras are **mammals**. Female zebras usually have one baby at a time. Baby zebras are called foals (FOHLS). At birth, they weigh 55 to 90 pounds (25 to 41 kg).

A foal drinks its mother's milk for about one year. It also starts eating grass as soon as a few days after it is born.

Baby zebras grow fast. They can gain one pound (.5 kg) a day for their first few months.

Most zebras are born white with brown stripes. They change color as they grow.

A young foal follows its mother around. Early on, it learns to recognize the pattern of stripes on her rear.

Foals form very strong bonds with their mothers. Mothers show them what to eat, where to find food, and how to watch for predators.

Fathers usually do not help raise foals. But, young male plains zebras are sometimes close to their fathers. By watching their fathers, they learn how to **protect** their family group. Foals leave their family group after one to four years.

Uncovered!

A foal can run with its mother about an hour after it is born. This helps it stay with its family group and escape predators.

Survivors

Life in Africa isn't easy for zebras. Besides natural predators, humans hunt them for their meat and fur. And, new buildings and farms take over their **habitats**.

Still, zebras **survive**. In fact, plains zebras can be found in large numbers. And, people work to save zebra habitats. Zebras help make Africa an amazing place!

Uncovered!

Mountain zebras are vulnerable. That means they are in some danger of dying out. Grevy's zebras are endangered. That means they are in great danger of dying out.

In the wild, zebras live about 25 years.

Masalala!

I'll bet you never knew...

...that zebras see very well. In fact, many scientists believe that zebras can see in the dark as well as owls!

...that zebras roll in dirt and mud to get clean. After a good roll, they shake off the dirt and mud to get rid of loose skin and hairs. Dirt and mud also **protect** zebras from bug bites and sunburn.

...that zebras are drawn to almost anything with black and white stripes! If stripes are painted on a wall, most zebras will stand near it.

Important Words

communicate (kuh-MYOO-nuh-kayt) to share knowledge, thoughts, or feelings.

continent one of Earth's seven main land areas.

groom to clean and care for.

habitat a place where a living thing is naturally found.

herbivore (HUHR-buh-vawr) an animal that eats plants.

mammal a member of a group of living beings. Mammals make milk to feed their babies and usually have hair or fur on their skin.

plateau (pla-TOH) a raised area of flat land.

protect (pruh-TEHKT) to guard against harm or danger.

social (SOH-shuhl) naturally living or growing in groups.

survive to continue to live or exist.

Web Sites

To learn more about zebras, visit ABDO Publishing Company online. Web sites about zebras are featured on our Book Links page. These links are routinely monitored and updated to provide the most current information available.

www.abdopublishing.com

Index